THE EYE OF THE NEEDLE

retold and illustrated by Teri Sloat

based on a Yupik tale as told by Betty Huffman

DUTTON CHILDREN'S BOOKS   NEW YORK

Library of Congress Cataloging-in-Publication Data

Sloat, Teri.

   The eye of the needle/retold and illustrated by Teri Sloat.—
1st ed.

      p.   cm.

   ''Based on a Yupik tale as told by Betty Huffman.''

   Summary: Sent out by his grandmother to find food, Amik consumes
a series of animals of ever-increasing size and brings back more than
he thinks.

   ISBN 0-525-44623-0

   1. Yupik Eskimos—Legends.   [1. Yupik Eskimos—Legends.
2. Eskimos—Alaska—Legends.   3. Indians of North America—Alaska—
Legends.]   I. Title.

E99.E7S52   1990   89-49476

398.2'089971—dc20   CIP

[E]   AC

Published in the United States by
Dutton Children's Books,
a division of Penguin Books USA Inc.

Designer: Riki Levinson

First Edition   10 9 8 7 6 5 4 3 2 1

to Betty Huffman, my favorite storyteller

Long ago, on the shore of the cold sea, Little Amik lived with his grandmother in a tiny sod hut.

It was the time between the dark of winter and the warmth of summer, and there was little left to eat. Amik and his grandmother waited for the sun to melt the ice and for the spring breeze to send it from the shore. Then they could gather food from the sea once again.

Grandmother sat inside the hut, sewing with a beautiful ivory needle. Her eyes were old, but the wide, open eye of her needle helped her see many things.

One day, when Grandmother knew the ice was ready to leave, she spoke.

"Little Amik, I have been watching you grow. This spring, you are big enough to go out and hunt our food for us."

The next morning, Amik dressed quickly in his newly mended spring parka and hurried to the shore.

In a stream trickling past his feet, something flickered across the pebbles. Amik scooped up a tiny needlefish.

"I am so hungry," he said. "I will eat this and catch something bigger for Grandmother." And with that ...

... he popped the spiny
needlefish into his mouth.
"Glump."
Down
went the
needlefish.
A moment later, Amik
said, "I am still hungry."

As Amik followed the shore, a squirmy hooligan fish flopped at his feet. He reached into the water and grabbed its slippery sides.

"I am so hungry," he said. "I will eat this and catch something bigger for Grandmother." And with that ...

"Gulump."
  Down
      slipped the
          hooligan.

But a moment later, Amik said, "I am still hungry."

A few steps ahead, noisy seagulls swooped over salmon in a little river.

Amik scattered the birds with a handful of pebbles. Catching a salmon by the tail, he licked his lips and said, "I am *so* hungry. I will eat this and catch something bigger for Grandmother." And with that...

Amik opened his mouth wide and...

"GULLUMP."
   Down
      slid the
         salmon.
But only a moment later, he said, "I am STILL hungry!"

Amik hurried along the beach, eating more and more but growing hungrier and hungrier.

Soon he came upon a fat seal resting on the sand. Amik thought how his grandmother loved seal. But he said, "I am SO hungry. I will eat this and catch something bigger for Grandmother." And with that...

...he lifted the seal, stretched his mouth open wide, and ...

"GULLUMMP!"

Down
    flipped the
        seal.

But within a moment, Amik said, "I am STILL hungry!"

And on down the beach he went, in search of more food.

Not far ahead, a lazy
walrus slept on the rocks,
basking in the warm sun.
Amik crept up close.

While the walrus slept, Amik grasped him by his long, ivory tusks. "Grandmother would be proud of this catch," he said. "But I am SO hungry. I will wait to catch something even bigger for Grandmother." And with that...

He lifted the walrus from the rocks, opened his mouth wider than ever, and...

"GULLUUMMP!"
        Down
            wriggled the
                walrus.

After he jiggled the walrus into a comfortable spot, Amik said, "I am STILL hungry!"

Out on the water, Amik saw the prize of the sea, a great whale! Here was a creature with enough meat to feed an entire village for a whole winter. To Amik the whale looked very tasty indeed.

Amik watched the whale glide in on the crest of a wave. "I am so hungry," he said, without one thought of his grandmother. And with that...

He bent down low and opened his mouth to an enormous size. When the wave rolled in to crash on the sand...

"G-U-L-L-U-U-M-M-P!"
Down
rushed the
WHALE!

After a moment, Amik said, "I am NOT hungry!"

"But I AM very thirsty."
Stopping at the nearest
stream, he slurped swallow
after swallow until the
stream was dry.

Then Amik took a long,
long rest.

When he awoke, Amik remembered he had saved nothing for his grandmother.

Too tired and much too full to hunt, Amik plodded slowly back to the hut, wondering what to tell Grandmother.

When Grandmother heard Amik outside, she called, "Come in with your catch, Amik. I am *so* hungry."

Amik was very uncomfortable. "But, Grandmother, my catch is much too big to bring through the door."

Grandmother was sewing with her ivory needle. "You must have returned with many things for us, Amik. Climb to the top of the hut and come in through the smoke hole."

Amik knew the smoke hole was much smaller even than the doorway. But he always did what his grandmother told him, so he pulled himself to the top of the hut before he asked, "How am I to squeeze through such a small hole?"

"Now you can come in through the eye of my needle," she replied.

Amik groaned. "Grandmother, the eye of your needle is many times smaller than the smoke hole."

But as soon as Grandmother held the needle up to the smoke hole, Amik was magically drawn into the hut.

As he slid through the
needle into the hut, there
was a loud "POP!" Then
a rush of water swirled
him around and around.

Out can

"SWISH!" Out slipped th

"SWOOSH!" Out slid the salmon.

"SPLASH!" Out flipped the seal.

"WHOOSH!" Out wriggled the walrus.

...e needlefish, past Grandmother's nose.

...ooligan fish.

And they all flowed out of the hut.

Then with a great "RUMBLE!"...
out on a wave rolled the whale.

Out of the whale came shrimp, seaweed, crabs, fish eggs,

and even a whaling ship in full sail.

When everything came to rest, Grandmother said, "Amik, what a wonderful provider you are."

Grandmother enjoyed a fine feast. Then she proudly shared their catch with all who came to see them. Amik did not eat—he was no longer hungry.